The effects of Media violence on children and Teenagers

Teddy Kelemwork

Media Maniac Copyright © 2009 by Teddy Kelemaork. All rights reserved Printed in the United States of America. No part of this book may be reproduced or transmitted in any form or by any means, electronic or mechanical, including photocopying, recording, or by any information storage and retrieval system, without written permission from the publisher. For information,

info@MotivationalToday.com   www.MotivationalToday.com

First Edition

ISBN: 1449913970

Dedication

I dedicate this book to my beautiful daughter Kerta F. Theodros. I wish your generation becomes better than the current one. I'm working hard to create a beautiful world that you can embrace and enjoy. You are my life and I love you.

Acknowledgements

First of all I would like to thank God for all my success, without whom I would not be able to breathe this air. I like to thank my families as well as Dr. Jeffery Goldhagen, Dr. Benjamin Piper and Dr. Assegid W. Habtewold for all the contribution and constant encouragement in my journey. You stood by me supporting my projects and goals. I can't thank you enough for being so kind. I would like to honor my mentor Janine Driver, The Body Language Expert who motivated me and trained me as an expert in the public speaking and nonverbal communication world. Congratulations on your success of "You Say More than You think". Your dynamic personality will always encourage me. I would like to thank Jerusalem Merkebu who was my Senior Research Assistant and Dean of Admissions at Zadock University. You have been a blessing from God himself. You have a special calling in your life and I am blessed to be a part of that journey.

Foreword

The 21st C (aka information age) brought to us both opportunities and challenges. This era appears a blessing in disguise for mankind. Since we joined the new millennium, information and media technologies become more affordable and accessible than ever. No question that we are enjoying the fruits of this advancement.

However, even if we benefited so much from the mushrooming of technologies, we are caught by surprise to find ourselves victims of our own making. The negative impact of media is more severe and consequential when it affects the new generation- children and teens. Because of its seriousness, many people from all walks of life and all over the world expressed their concern. Many experts spoke out the negative implications of uncensored exposure of children and teens towards violent media. Parents around the world publicly expressed their frustrations, anger, and helplessness about media impact against their children.

Someone, nevertheless, went beyond showing grieve concern about the negative influence of violent media against children and teens. Out of his longstanding passion and compassion towards helping teens, Teddy-a youth pastor for so many good years, came up with an educational and instructional call to action book entitled "Media Maniac: The effects of Media violence on children and Teenagers". Observing first hand destructive effects of ill-media towards children and teens, he trod upon a very demanding road- a path that requires intense research and dedication to identify the underlining problems and uncover possible solutions in combating the acute and chronic sequels of media against the future generation- children and teens.

Therefore, this book is a product of genuine care from a responsible individual who vowed to save the future generation. The book is systematically divided into three parts: Impact of Media Violence on the Child Psyche, Solutions for Media Violence, and The Benefit of Using Rating. The first section provided the essential background information that showed how the physiological development of children and teens brain lacks to understand good and wrong decisions and actions. This part gives adequate insights for parents and all concerned parties to understand that the victims are helpless, in most parts, to protect themselves from the invading media. The second section deals with possible solutions in fighting the consequences of ill-media towards children and teens. The third part recommends the need to rate and filter before allowing teens to watch some media outlets. I found the last part very important especially for those countries that don't enforce such preventive mechanisms.

This book provides lots of valuable data, practical examples, and solutions to combat violence influenced by media. Besides, the results of many studies that correlated the influence of violent media against children and teens are covered in this book. Most importantly, the book lift off the blame from children and teens because they are victims of their own prematurity by arguing that immature brain of teenagers gets motivated towards violence. Teddy argues, "At no point in time can we actually blame the teenagers for the violence they may be inflicting on others due to the violence they have been observing in the television shows and movies". The author emphasized that Teens cannot control their impulses; neither can differentiate between good and evil. These kinds of data packed in this book redirect the fingers pointed at teens as the source of violence into inspiring all stakeholders to get involved and render hand in preventing violent media from denying us of the next generation with attached costly prices. The book also emphasized that intoxications and addictions can lead teens' brain into the path of destruction. The book is filled with lots of captivating incidents influenced by violent media, for example, the tragic one in Columbine High School. I also found the book very helpful for policy makers and all stakeholders who should read and understand the immediate and long term impact of ill-media against teens and what they should do about it. Libraries should also make copies of this book available so that teens themselves understand what is going on and be part of the solution. I also recommend elementary and high schools consider the book as one of their book reading list.

Assegid W. Habtewold (DMV, MSC)

President and CEO, Success Pathways, LLC
Founder, PRO Leadership Global, Inc
Candidate for Doctor of Strategic Leadership,

Table of Content

Introduction   9

Chapter 1: Impact of Media Violence on the Child Psyche   10

- Brain Development in Teenagers   10
- Brain Functions in teenagers   12
- How the immature brain of teenagers gets motivated toward violence   20
- Movies & TV   28
- Music   32
- Computer and video games   36

Chapter 2: Solutions for Media Violence   49

- Factors That Promote Violence   55
- Is Violence Inherent?   60

Chapter 3: The Benefit of Using Rating   67

- The Rating System   71
- Filtering   73

Conclusion   80

Bibliography   82

Introduction:

Teenagers are considered as the most sensitive age groups, due to both psychological and physiological changes that they undergo. It has been observed recently that violence portrayed in the media is having prolonged and dangerous effects on the mind of the teenagers. The most significant are those that are carried across through television programs, movies and computer games. They create a long lasting negative impact on the psyche of the teenagers; making them suicidal or criminal minded. It is highly unfortunate when they end up being a hapless victim of the ravaging violence through media onslaught and cease to be an asset to human society.

The modern society is experiencing a bad phase of violence and bloodshed everywhere. In spite of much instability all around, the portrayal of violence on television shows, movies, computer games, as well as music goes on un-interrupted, leading to further complications. Our future generation is growing up in an atmosphere of violence and bloodshed.

Chapter 1: Impact of Media Violence on Child Psyche

The teenagers are exposed to media violence of various types like never before, with an easy accessibility of a variety of media forms to more and more people. In this chapter we will briefly discuss how the various forms of media are having a negative impact on the psyche of teenagers in particular and society in general. However, before getting into a detailed discussion about that, it is important to understand the pattern of brain development in teenagers.

Brain development in teenagers

The functional ability of a teen brain differs from that of an adult brain. The teenage brain is still in a developing state. Consequently, it performs or acts like a set of loose wires. It ponders over things that arrests its attention, makes decisions (more often than not impulsive) and evaluates choices that a situation presents, and so on. It does everything but, with a lack of integration, balance, and poise.

The important segments of the brain - prefrontal cortex, synapses, myelin, and nucleus accumbency, and others - work in perfect symmetry and assist an adult in making astute decisions and treading the path of righteousness and justice. These processes are not yet developed in a teenager. For instance, the prefrontal cortex in the teenage state slowly learns its natural functions such as measuring outcomes of an act, curbing impulses, taking control of the activities and realizing the true characteristics of the people they are coming in contact with, and so on. In the process of teenage brain development, synapses and myelin play vital roles. Since these three vital segments are still in a dormant state in terms of utilizing their full capacity, a teen brain is not equipped to make appropriate decisions when it comes to choosing between what is good and what is bad. [1]

Brain Functions in teenagers

To grasp a clear concept of the inter relation between the four key areas of brain and teen behavior you need to know the functions of these brain parts well. Let us probe into it and get to know the functions of these brain parts one after the other.

Prefrontal Cortex- Prefrontal Cortex is a complex brain part with a lot of responsible functions to perform. It is actually the innermost part of the frontal Lobe. This specific term was brought in by Richard Owen in 1868. Important sub divisions of this brain part are - Orbitofrontal, Frontopolar, Posterior Dorsolateral, Mid-Dorsolateral, Ventrolateral, Ventromedial, Basal and Orbital. This particular segment of your brain is known to perform executive functions and helps an individual in differentiating between good and evil. It designs cognitive behavior of an individual, and makes him or her focus on the possible consequences of what the individual is doing presently. Prefrontal Cortex also makes the social behavior perfect and sharpens the decision making skills. A well balanced Prefrontal Cortex will help you express yourself much better, and enable you to make your personality pleasing. Not only that, Prefrontal Cortex also controls the feelings of remorse or guilt in a person. The following disorders arise out of irregular Prefrontal Cortex functions in an individual. It

- Creates problems in the brain imaging system.
- Create problems in the nerve linkage systems.
- Lead to severe troubles such as extreme stress, depression etc. People who suffer from the malfunction of the Prefrontal Cortex are more prone to committing suicide or becoming drug addict.
- Creates problem in the connection among the frontal lobes.

Thus Prefrontal Cortex plays an important role in ascertaining the psyche of a teen age boy or a girl. As this highly crucial part is still in the process of shaping up, it exposes the teenagers more towards danger as they do not possess the ability to fully understand the importance or threat of the situation they are in. [2]

Synapses - Synapses, one of the most important brain parts, act as neural junctions for maintaining a steady communication process between neurons. Based on proper functioning of synapses, your brain and your nervous system can communicate with all the important body parts and thus establish a strong control over them.

Synapses are also referred to as chemical synapses, electrical synapses or immunological synapses. With the help of Synapses or chemical synapses, neurons can emit signals to each other, and also communicate signals to other important parts of the body like muscles or glands etc. It is because of these synapses that neurons become capable of shaping up circuits within the Central Nervous System. Based on the circuits that synapses create in the Central Nervous System, the brain is able to perceive and think easily.

Mal functioning of Synapses can give rise to different sorts of physical disorders in the teens. Teens can be subject to -

- Eating disorder

- Dismennoreah
- Attention deficit hyperactivity disorder
- Obsessive compulsive disorder
- Dysthymia [3]

Myelin - Myelin is the third important segment of the four major areas of brain. This crucial segment of brain was discovered in 1854. It is an electrically insulating substance. The basic ingredients that actually are found inside Myelin are as follows – myelin basic protein, proteolipid proteins, lipid, galactocelebroside, glycolipid and myelin oligodendrocyte glycoprotein. Myelin which is an outgrowth of a glial cell is known as the most salient feature of the vertebrates.

In order to maintain the functionalities and efficacy of the Central Nervous System in proper order, the proper and effective functioning of Myelin is a must. As a matter of fact, Myelin is capable of creating a layer around the axon of a neuron. This particular layer created by Myelin is known as Myelin Sheath. This specific layer or Myelin Sheath guards the nervous system and helps it to maintain proper functioning. In the aspect of maturity this particular brain part is truly significant. The sole responsibility of Myelin Sheath is increasing the speed of different types of impulses. These impulses are effectively communicated along the myelinated fiber. These impulses can also make their way through the unmyelinated fibers, though the tempo or speed in this case would be much slower than their passage through myelinated fibers. Apart from that Myelin also helps axons to preserve and smoothly run electrical currents.

Lack of myelin or imbalance in the entire process of myelination might result in troublesome abnormalities especially the Schizophrenia syndrome. Apart from that there can be other serious problems like dyslexia. [4]

Nucleus Accumbens- Nucleus Accumbens is the last one of these four key areas of your brain and actually denote a collection of neurons. There are two sub divisions for Nucleus Accumbens – Nucleus Accumbens Core and Nucleus Accumbens Shell. Nucleus Accumbens are found in each side of the brain. The other terms by which this specific brain part is commonly known are – Nucleus Accumbens Septi and Accumbens Nucleus. Nucleus Accumbens is situated in a very important position of the brain. It is placed at the joint where the Putamen and the head of the caudate meet.

Nucleus Accumbens play a crucial role both in the immature teen brain as well as the adult brain. This particular brain segment is responsible for extreme reactions to excitement, pleasure, threat or fear, placebo medical procedures, laughter as well as rewards. To control the excitement level or maintain childish fun and frolic at a harmless level, this particular brain part contributes a lot.

The function ability of Nucleus Accumbens is a bit slow in teens. So, if the teen or adolescent gets prone to fatal addictions like excessive smoking, drug addictions or even alcoholism, their addiction would have a violent and negative impact on the Nucleus Accumbens. Because of this harmful addiction the dopamine level swells up a lot in the Nucleus Accumbens. It harshly reflects in many negative behaviors in the teens. Lack of balance or excess of this ingredient can lead your child to fatal and violent acts. [5]

A very good example to substantiate the above point of view is the incident at Columbine High School. Two teenagers suddenly opened fire and started to hurl bombs. The whole incident killed several students and teachers of the school and many more were injured. The boys might have had a prior influence of violence in their life through movies or video games, but it was an accepted notion that the boys were inspired and influenced by the movie named Matrix to undertake such an act. The boys were not even remorseful for what they had done because of getting used to watching violence and blood in the movies and television shows.

Exposure to media violence influences the teenage minds, and they display aggression in their behavior. There is a desire to harm others, which starts with a *mere* shove and fight. Getting accustomed to regular acts of violence in real lives, has led us to overlook them, and more often than not incidents of teenage violence are presented as sensational events by the media.

These children are victims to abnormal psychological behavior that get manifested in their later lives.

A senior scientist at the University of Michigan's Institute of Social Research, Leonard Eron carried out a study on eight-hundred and fifty-six subjects. Their aggression levels were monitored since they were eight years old. The levels were rated by the peers of the subjects and a direct relation was observed between the levels and the amount of exposure to media violence. The period was segregated into eight, ten, nineteen and thirty years of age. The co-relation between violence and aggression was directly proportional. They were manifested through the development of anti-social attitude and enhanced usage of abusive language. [6]

At no point in time can we actually blame the teenagers for the violence they may be inflicting on others due to the violence they have been observing in the television shows and movies. In most cases, it has been found out that they are unable to differentiate between the real world and the virtual world and, thus, end up as a confused person hanging in between the two worlds.

How Immature Brain of Teenagers Get Motivated Toward Violence

Teenage is considered an age of inflamed passion. At this crucial phase of life, immaturity plays a crucial role in the teenage brain development process. Things said, heard or spoken leave an unfathomable impact on teen psychology. Media today is such a phenomenon that can easily entangle a teen brain with an unprecedented sweep.

A teen falls into such a trap easily at a rate much faster than an adult, as the Prefrontal Cortex, the area right behind the forehead, is less functional in a teen age boy or girl. Prefrontal Cortex the vital part necessary for decision making remains at a formative stage, the obvious outcome of which is the inability of a teen to decide about the moral code of behaviors in many situations. They cannot control their impulses; neither can differentiate between good and evil. They are also unable to decide where exactly to draw the line, when they get involved into a thing, be it a relation or something exciting. Lack of regular functioning of the Prefrontal Cortex make them lag behind in important aspects like- goal or priority setting, implementation of planning, and organizing capability. At this age they lack in rational thinking capability, which often leads them to perform acts of violence just for the sake of experience a lot of thrill. Thus they land up in trouble, as they do not have the far fetched sight to see the outcome of such an act.

Other aspects too act as instigators leading to violence. Teens are involved in acts of violence at this age as they harbor a very strong aptitude for risky and rebellious acts. They are not conscientious of whether the act is right or wrong. They just wish to experience adventure even at the cost of someone else's trouble. The teenager does bear a sensitive zeal toward rewards or appreciations, and to achieve a different status in comparison to others in the group, they can go to any extent, and be ready for any amount of risk.

That is why in this particular phase, a teenager is like an emotional time bomb. When they are looking up for something that matches their interest level in various media forms like TV, video games, and the Internet, what they usually find as a match is violence. Based on the immaturity factor of their brains, they cannot resist the negative aspects. That is why in most cases, these negatives invade their immature brains and get them involved in acts in which they should otherwise never have entangled themselves. [7]

Apart from the media playing a crucial role in instigating violence amongst teenagers, which leaves a strong impact on the immature brain, the potential reason behind teen violence is fear. It has been noticed that a child or a teenager when threatened by an external atmosphere, can react in a weird manner. The feeling of being surrounded by an uncertain situation seeming a threat to the teenager, can lead them to commit a violent act. This happens because it seems as the only measure to the teen to ward off the feeling of the inherent emotional insecurity. The expression of sheer strength seems to be the only mode of making him or her secure.

External intoxication or addiction can lead a teen brain into the path of destruction. Alcoholism, drug addiction like cocaine, brown sugar, heroine etc. kills the capacity of rational thinking. If a teenager gets into this addiction nothing can be worse than that. Myelination plays a vital role for maintaining a level of stability in teen brains or to turn them towards acts of violence. The Myelin Sheath which covers up the neurons or axons of brain cells lets electrical impulses travel in a much faster rate. Based on that, the brain as well as the nervous system can co ordinate or connect with the rest of the body parts in a much faster way. Now what happens in case of a teen is, the Myelin Sheath does not get mature enough to perform with its full strength. Through brain scan researches in the University of California at Los Angeles, it has been found out that, teen brains in the age group of 12-16 years show less Myelin development rather than young people of age group 23-30 years.

One significant part of a teen brain plays a great role in instigating a teen to act out of the way leading him/her to end up in some kind of violent act. This specific part of the brain is known as Limbic Area, and its sole job is to excite emotional reactions. The emotional reactions triggered by this particular area of the brain, can entrap a teenager into a situation of potential threat. The instigation that the teenagers receive from this part of the brain does not let them think of the impending danger. All that they long for is, enjoying the thrill associated with the act, encouraging the teenager to develop a do or die attitude in situations where it is not at all required. A small part of the Limbic Area known as Amygdale plays a significant role in shaping up this daring attitude in the teens.

This theory has been successfully proved at Harvard's McLean Hospital. An efficient team of doctors under the deft leadership of Dr. Deborah Yurgelun had carried out an experiment in this regard. On the final stage of the research, they found that when it comes to processing emotions, the front lobes of an adolescent is less active compared to an adult, whereas the Amygdale was much more active in the adolescents or teens. The research proved that the emotional side is much stronger in a teen rather than the rational side of their brain activities. So it becomes clear that it is Amygdale that has a major role to play when a teenager gets involved in a risky venture or commits some dangerous and violent act. [8]

Teenagers tend to show instances of immaturity as well as frustrating teenage behavior, chiefly based upon the mixed reaction of a less functional prefrontal cortex and a highly functional nucleus accumbens, which always unfailingly excites a teen mind to seek things that are pleasurable, rewarding, and in appreciation of their valor. It is the impact of nucleus accumbens that prevents their mind from considering whether they are doing something wrong or right. That is why it has been the teenagers only, who are more prone to lethal addictions like drugs or alcohol and even hidden sexual behaviors. The basic reason working behind this is their unfailing craving for non-stop excitement, adventure, and limitless fun. [9]

The emotional changes that take place when a child or a teenager is experiencing violence in real life, and in movies or television shows are different. They are more scared of violence in reality than on the screen. However, constant exposure to violence on screen changes the emotional reactions of the children and teenagers. Gradually, they stop showing any difference in their emotional reaction to the violence on screen and in real life, clearly points out that children and teenagers are actually losing the ability to distinguish between real life and the virtual life.

The acceptability of violence in the society to a certain amount enhances the complexity of the situation in the form of a belief, that 'violence is unavoidable'. This is termed as the "Mean World" syndrome. It is public fear of lack of security, where there is a perception that crime is present everywhere. They end up overestimating the risk of becoming victims of crime, and that the neighborhoods have ceased to be safe. There is always an assumption that the crime curve is on a perpetual rise even when the crime rate is not really increasing. Here, the fear of crime comes across as a serious personal problem. A study by George Gerbner is the longest running study that deals with youth behavior and television violence. The research concluded that excessive television viewing leads children to perceive that the real world is akin to the images they watch on television.

The Kaiser Family Foundation conducted a study in 2003. Forty-seven percent of the parents in this study revealed that children belonging to the age group four to six imitate aggressive behavior from watching television. Even the new media is found to render a similar impact on the developing child psyche. Another study by Craig Anderson and Brad Bushman of the Iowa State University in 2003 reported, children playing violent video games even for a short time period show aggression in their regular behaviors. [10]

As they recognize the acceptability of violence in the television shows and movies, they start believing that violence in any form is acceptable. The whole mental setup of a child or a teenager slowly changes to a violence-based setup, leading the child or the teenager to believe that violence is the best way to get something or put up a protest. Growing up with a violent attitude, poses a real threat to the future, generating more unrest and destruction for these future citizens of the world. [11]

Thus, when an immature teen brain comes in contact with violence portrayed through different media channels the negative impact gets radiated into them easily. There might be some teens with inherent violent sparks in them, though not all are alike. However, continual watching of violence tends to turn even the least violent teen into one relishing in violent acts because of the immaturity of the brain.

Movies & TVs

This section deals with a very interesting study conducted on a group of university students, divided into two equal subgroups. One subgroup was exposed to violent movies and television shows for a period of three weeks; and the other subgroup was exposed to non-violent movies and television shows for the same period of time. Throughout the week, the subgroups were not allowed to interact with each other. When the period of three week was over, the students belonging to both the subgroups were asked to apply for the university courses of their choice. But wherever they applied, their application was rejected intentionally, to observe their pattern of reaction. It was observed that students watching the violent movies and television shows reacted in a very violent manner, compared to the students exposed to non-violent movie and television shows.

In 2000, the US Congress was presented with a joint statement by the American Academy of Pediatrics and American Academy of Child and Adolescent Psychiatry that had a reference of over a thousand studies conducted by doctors, psychologists and child psychiatrics. Restriction to exposure of violence on movies and television would reduce the violence and aggression in behavior. Less TV viewing results in lesser violence. This is demonstrated by the Stanford University study. If the kids are encouraged to turn off the televisions and video games, there will be almost a fifty percent decrease in verbal aggression and forty percent decrease in physical aggression. The researchers had two San Jose elementary schools as their subjects. The kids belonged to third and forth grades. Half of the kids' per week television viewing hours were restricted to less than seven for twenty weeks and two-thirds of them participated in a ten-day period to turn off television completely. The results revealed that the children who were the most aggressive during the onset of the study showed visible improvement in their behavior. The overall data also reported reduction in obesity too. [12]

This study clearly proves that violence depicted in television shows and movies have a negative impact on the teenage mind. The vulnerable mind of the teenagers is severely affected by the external changes taking place around them. Positive changes leave a positive effect on their minds, while negative incidents leave a negative effect.

The easy access of teenagers to television sets and film DVDs at home or visiting the next door movie theatres is a common phenomenon. The predominance of violence in the visual media has made them an easy prey for media violence. As violence is the most watched category in any visual medium and the most selling after sex, the producers of movies and television shows use violence as much as possible to draw in audience; the soft target of which invariably happen to be the teenagers. They get easily attracted towards violence portrayed on the television shows and movies, tending to believe in them and apply them in practical life. There begins the real problem, as they start to live a very unreal life in the real world.

Studies conducted the world over to find out the effects of movie and television violence on a child's or teenager's mind, have presented alarming results. On an average count, within the one hour "prime time" slot as denoted in television lingo, nearly fifty crimes and twelve murders were depicted in the various shows being aired. [13] The alarming fact is, within that one hour, more than seventy percent of the teenagers and children across USA were watching these television shows, with or without their parents' company. It should be remembered that the effects of such programs and shows on the mind of a mature adult and that of a teenager is not the same.

In most cases, experiencing violence through the television shows becomes a habit, which gradually turns into addiction for the teenagers. No amount of cajoling or coercion works to prevent the child from completing the day without watching shows steeped in violence. This leads them to believe that behaving in a violent way is correct. They begin to react violently at any given opportunity, creating uneasiness and unrest not only in their own minds but, within his/her family and the society as a whole. [14]

Movies, being an important form of entertainment have a tremendous social impact, as they are watched by people belonging to all age groups. In reality, these teenagers and children do not watch only movies that are rated suitable for them. On the contrary, they have an attraction toward extremely violent movies. In the movie Robocop, a total of thirty-two deaths are shown. The sequel of this movie had portrayed eighty-one killings. These movies are very popular among children and teenagers, which clearly emphasizes how brutally they are exposed to violence. This renders an obvious negative impact on their psyche.

Music

Music is an inseparable part of human civilization. As music has a soothing effect on the mind and the soul, it is being used effectively for healing, treatment and relaxation purposes. Apart from this, there is something more to the relationship between music and humans, which is really disturbing. During the last decade, several studies linking violent behaviors with listening to certain types of music were conducted with many groups of people, especially teenagers. This worrying development redrew the whole picture of the relationship between people and music. There has been a constant change in the way music is created and presented before the audience. In the past, one used to hear music. But today, we not only just *hear* music; we are simultaneously entertained with certain visuals along with the music, such as the music video. It has been observed many a times that a good deal of derogatory, objectionable, or sexual terms is being used in the lyrics of songs. Albums of Eminem, Dr. Dre and Limp Bizkit have been enlisted by the world's largest music company, The Universal Music Group for containing mysogynism and violence in their lyrics. Graphic violence was a major part of Madonna's 2002 video titled "What It Feels Like For a Girl". [15]

In many cases, the music videos are found to contain objectionable sexual content which may not be suitable for child or teenage viewing. All these words and images render a negative impact on the psyche of the teenagers and it is also bringing about unusual changes in their behavioral patterns. This may lead to further problems, as the teenagers may become criminal minded or destructive in nature and eventually evolve as a potential danger for human society.

Many experts are of the opinion that music does play a very significant and important role in the overall mental setup of a child or teenager. Since the child or the teenager is in a developing state, he or she will be affected by anything and everything that catches his/her imagination. Music is one such thing that can attract the mind of a child or teenager very easily. In many cases, you will find that the lyrics or the music videos are such that it excites the mind of a teenager or a child to take up some violent acts, which otherwise he would not have done. In many cases it has been observed that many teenagers have their first fight with friends under the influence of the contents of the music videos.

We also find that many teenagers and children have role models when it comes to music. They are addicted to listening to the songs of some particular band or performer. They are inclined to imitate the actions of the performer and passionately follow the lyrics of these songs. If they idolize the wrong singer or band, they might begin to imitate the actions that may not be socially acceptable. But this may not make much difference to them, as they lose the sense of right and wrong. They have a feeling that whatever their idol is doing or saying is the correct way of looking at and leading life. This may lead to severe problems for the teenager or the child as he or she grows up. [16]

There is an important issue evolving out of this discussion. It is a common question where people want to know, whether wrong music can create a killer out of a young mind. The answer cannot be a straight yes or no. Things are not that simple. But it is true that music has an everlasting effect on the mind of a teenager.

Computer and Video games

A present day teenager has no dearth of entertainment options. He does not have to leave his house in order to enjoy himself and have fun. In his own room, he can spend hours having fun by playing computer and video games. The computer and video games have taken the home gaming world by storm. Both these segments are one of the fastest developing in the world and each day, new games are getting added to the list. The games come under various purposes, from educational to just sheer entertainment. But statistical data suggest, the most sold computer and video games are those which contain elements of violence and sex in it.

Nearly fifty percent of the users of these computer and video games are those who belong to the age group of twelve to twenty years old. In the recent past, there has been substantial increase in teenage violence and one of the major reasons is attributed to the ill effect of computer and video games. Many studies conclude that both computer and video games create more adverse effects in the mind of a teenager than television shows or movies. In case of television shows and movies, the teenager is just a recipient of the action and he has no role to play – rather he or she just sits and watches. At the most, the teenager can imagine a lot of things which are influenced by the television shows or the movies at a later time.

But in the case of computer and video games, the teenager is not only the watcher, but he or she is also the doer. He becomes an active participant. Let us consider an example of a game involving shooting with a pistol and killing enemies. In this game, the teenager is provided with a virtual gun in his hand and he can shoot the enemies in the virtual world of the internet or video game. He will be also watching the whole event on the computer or television screen. Thus, he gets used to the idea of shooting and killing people with his own hands, as that is precisely the thing that he/she is doing virtually while playing the game. Once he/she gets addicted to such gaming actions, his mentality may start to change. This might well give rise to his/her desire to try out something similar in real life. Here exactly lies the danger of the ill effects of the computer and video games. [17]

There have been many instances where the teenagers have reacted in a way that is actually an extension of the manner in which they play their video and computer games. In London, two seventeen year-olds started to shoot at each other, in a similar fashion as they would have done in video or computer game. This happened in 2008. In that cross fire, on a street at New Cross, a woman named Magda Pnieswaka was shot in her head. Magda, twenty-six, was a nurse in a nursing home at Manley court. She was trapped in the cross fire and died immediately. She was the innocent victim of a violent act of two teenagers, who were not bothered of using a hand gun in public.[18]

There is no end to such kind of ruthless instances. Teenagers are actually becoming more restless and they are trying to enact in real life what that they are so used to in the virtual life. An important segment of computer and video games are related to sexual contents. In this case also, these games sell a lot more than other educational and soft games. The result is again very dangerous for both the individual and society. Teenagers become engrossed playing games with overt sexual contents.

But in most cases, the teenager does not have the sensitivity or maturity to handle this kind of content and game. So the natural fallout is that the games become their addiction and leads to perversion. There are many recent and past cases that help us to understand the extent to which teenagers can go once they are addicted to sexual contents.

In October 2009, four teenagers aged fifteen, sixteen, seventeen and nineteen were charged with gang raping a fifteen year old girl. The incident took place in Richmond, California. The police informed the press that nearly twenty people, all teenagers, attacked the girl, who was sitting in the school courtyard drinking alcohol. The attack had lasted for more than two hours. This incident is proving to us that teenagers are engrossed and used to sexual content in video and computer games, that they are not hesitant of converting their virtual actions into real life activities. This is a very worrying development in the modern society. [19]

A nearly similar incident took place in Hong Kong in 2008. Three teenagers were involved who were aged between sixteen and nineteen years in this gruesome act. They were charged with rape. They recorded the video footage of the rape and uploaded it into various websites over the Internet. This case is again testament to the growing perversion in the teenagers across the world as they found fun in shooting the whole episode and releasing it on the internet for others to enjoy. This is perversion at its worst. [20]

All these incidents are attributed to the growing inclusion of sexual contents in the computer and video games, which are being used by the teenagers all over the world. There is another aspect to this threat of video and computer games on teenagers of the present and coming generations. With the increase in the violence and sexual content in the games, patience and the sense of limitations are fading away from the minds of the teenagers. This in turn is leading to several other problems.

A recent incident that has taken place in October, 2009 is a glaring example of this problem. A seventeen year-old boy named James Callaghan was playing a computer game named

FIFA with his younger brother. James incidentally lost three consecutive games to his brother. This made him very angry. He went to the kitchen and picked up a kitchen knife, and then he went out of the house and picked up an axe. He went straight to the house of his neighbor where a sixty-five-year-old woman named Irene Roberton lived. James broke into the house and attacked the woman with the knife and axe. The old woman was struck six times on her head and stabbed several times on her back and stomach. She died on the spot. James also threatened many other teenage girls and few of his other neighbors who saw him returning from the house of Irene. [21]

This case is an example on how these computer games are really affecting the total mental makeup of a teenager and is wrecking havoc on the whole concept of community life. A recent study has revealed a lot more about the true nature of these computer and video games than we could have ever imagined. The study revealed that nearly ninety percent of the young American population plays computer and video games and out of them, nearly fifteen percent are severely addicted to these games. The addicted teenagers are in a position to do anything and everything in order to ensure that they get to play their games regularly. It is very similar to drug addiction. If the teenagers are stopped from playing these computer or video games, they may even end up killing someone!

A certain case that was included in this study, mentions a thirteen-year-old boy, who had the habit of playing computer games for more than twelve hours a day. The boy had said in an interview with the researchers that he felt suicidal.

It is also interesting to know that the United States Army uses video games such as Doom and Nintendo to train their people in the art of handling and using weapons. The same games are also available in the open market and many children and teenagers also play these games on a regular basis. So, one can easily infer that the games that are being used by the Army for shooting training purposes have to be very effective in that field. So, children and the teenagers are actually learning all about shooting from these games. This makes it all but natural that they would be interested in trying their shooting skills in real life situations. [22]

Here begins the problem. Once the children get addicted to bloodshed and violence, they will not be in a position to distinguish between the virtual world of the game and the real world. They end up with this crazy desire to press the trigger and revel when they see blood oozing out of their victims.

One of the very prominent examples to substantiate this issue is the shooting that took place in the Paducah area of Kentucky. The boy was only fourteen-years-old and he had never handled a real gun before; but he had played various shooting games for many years and had an idea of how to use a gun. He managed to fire not one or two, but eight shots and ended up shooting five on the head and the three other shots on the upper torso of his victims. All the eight children were fatally injured and died soon after. This incident points the extent of danger posed by these video and computer games containing violence and bloodshed as their primary elements. [23]

The Harvard Medical School has also done some very interesting studies in regard to computer games and teenage violence. One such study was concerned with Darren, a thirteen-year-old boy. Darren was a computer game addict and he loved to play games that had action and speed. One of his favorite games was Grand Theft Auto III. One day, Darren had a very bad time in school, as one of the teachers had scolded and embarrassed him in front of his classmates. Darren went back home with a very angry mind. He started the computer game Grand Theft Auto III; he blew up some cars and killed some people in the game. He also killed a woman in the game. Later Darren revealed that the woman in the game looked like the teacher who had insulted him. He felt satisfied at having killed her in the game. There is just one consolation in this case that Darren had actually shot the lady looking like her teacher in the game and did not think about doing it in real life. Else, there could have been another casualty. [24]

The negative effects of computer and video games are more than their positive impact. It is really a great challenge for parents and teachers to ensure that the teenagers stay away from the negative impact of such games.

Here are a series of questions that will help you recapitulate the contents of the above chapter.

Questionnaire

1. What are the four major components of teen brain development?

Answer: The four major components of teen brain development are Prefrontal Cortex, Synapses, Myelin and Nucleus Accumbens. These four segments play a vital role in the life of a teenager. Prefrontal Cortex helps an individual to decide what is right and what is wrong. Synapses and Myelin act like wires that maintain integrity in a teen brain. Nucleus Accumbens is the most powerful substance in a teen brain which always seeks pleasure and excitement.

2. Describe in brief the effects of the movies and television shows on the psyche of a teenager.

Answer: Movies and television shows are two of the most important ways of relaxation for the teenagers. They tend to watch television or go down to the nearest movie theatres whenever they have some free time. But at present we are experiencing a trend where the use of violence in the movies and the television shows are increasing with every passing day. This is rendering a negative impact on the minds of the teenagers as they try to imitate the violence. These usually get manifested in their impatience and urge to fulfill their desires at any given cost.

3. Do you think that music may have a bad affect on the mind of a child?

Answer: It is of common knowledge that music plays an important role in the overall mental build up of a person. The same holds true for a child. If the child is exposed to violent and vulgar music/albums, his mental development will also be affected by the same. This may lead to problems in his future and may create criminal or anti-social tendencies in that child.

4. Describe in brief how the computer and video games can be a source of concern for the proper development of a child.

Answer: Video and computer games are often referred to as one of the most important mediums of enjoyment and relaxation for a child. But at present, these two forms of relaxation and entertainment has become a source of headache for parents and teachers alike. In the present global market, we find that most of the video and computer games have some element of violence in it. In these games the gamer takes up the gun and shoots at others or do some other very violent act. These games make the child more prone and used to violence. It disturbs the mental balance of the child along with the social and community structure.

5. What is the relationship between violence and teen immaturity?

Answer: The aspect of teen immaturity is deeply related to the interrelationship of the brain segments. In a teenager, the Prefrontal Cortex is not in full swing. It remains in a formative stage. That is why; the teenagers are prone to taking impulsive decisions and making mistakes. Whereas Nucleus Accumbens, the most powerful brain part of a teen lead a teenager to do idiotic and often dangerous stuffs like violence. Because of these elements, an immature teen mind becomes susceptible to media violence at an alarming rate.

Chapter 2: Solutions for Media Violence

Violence is a far more complex factor to be explained by a single solution. The impact of violence on child and adolescent mind is myriad, depending on the immediate social surrounding of the individual. As the child becomes exposed to various media forms, more often than not, he comes across a common solution – violence is a sort of acceptable method to deal with problems. The situation that he is presented with is either imaginary or perceived reality. Be it newspapers, books, television, movies, video and computer games, or music, an adolescent mind has to deal with the impact of these mediums.

On an average, cartoons and commercials depict twenty-five violent acts every hour. [25] With a natural propensity to choose media figures as role models, children develop a tendency to enact the acts of violence in their real lives or in their minds. Both have a disastrous effect on their underdeveloped psyche. The impact is borne till he attains maturity and eventually they grow up with undesirable and disturbing character traits that render a different sort of impact in his social and personal relationships.

With the invasion of media on every aspect of our lives, there is a need to protect the tender minds of children from the violent content. Their limited apprehension faculties enhance their vulnerability. It therefore, becomes the responsibility of the adult members of the society to ensure that the children are able to enjoy the innocence of their growing up years and in the process also cultivate their senses to the realities of the society that they are a part of.

Media consumption actually occurs outside the school periphery. A child's immediate surrounding is his family. The onus thus lies with the members of the family to restrict and effectively transform the manner in which the child is exposed to the media. It is never possible to remove media presence from a child's life. But, the messages the children receive from the media needs to be monitored.

The parents can make it a point that there is no place for violence at home. The reading materials, TV and radio programs along with the games that the children regularly play can be monitored. Television being the most readily accessible media form arguably renders the maximum negative impact on a child's mind.

An audio-visual medium with images performing the violent acts in an identifiable set-up makes the child feel relative to the situation. It works to limit the television viewing hours to two or less, everyday. The parents can sit with the child and plan a weekly schedule of the programs to watch. After the selected programs get over, the set must be immediately turned off. The child must be taught to interpret the programs. This way they will be able to learn and identify the reality and the unreality of the situations depicted. It must also be made clear there is always an inevitable relation between the actions and the consequences. Promote television viewing as a family activity. The parents can sit with the children as they watch the programs and note the manner in which they comprehend and relate to the content. [26]

In a recent study, it has been observed that in the American society especially, the number hours the children spend before the television is followed only by another activity – sleeping! So monitoring media violence that emanates through television becomes much more important. But, before exercising control, there are certain aspects that need to be thought over.

Those programs that depict racist, stereotypes and sexist characters must be avoided. In order to seek effective solution to the rapid encroachment of the media violence, an important aspect needs to be kept in mind. Very often it is found that violence is presented in a camouflaged manner. This entails that there is not the usually gory look, but the impact rendered is extremely unnerving. Subtle expressions of violence like the manner in which a chauvinist attitude is presented, challenges the apprehensive limitations of a teenage mind. Therefore, they exhibit confused reactions to certain conditions.

Then again, violence is also presented in a fashion that can evoke laughter or humor. In each of these situations, it becomes imperative that the children are equipped to understand the criteria for desirable social behavior. They also need to be made aware that a certain set of social behavior is expected of them and it is in their best interest that they must to adhere to those norms. A child essentially begins to learn from his family. As the members of the family exercise a certain amount of caution in the manner in which they present themselves before the child, they will be able to control a lot of the negative impacts of media violence. If a child gets to learn what good humor is, he will automatically learn that it is never desirable to make fun at other's sufferings. [27]

He must also be taught the concept of power and strength and the manner in which they ought to be manifested. They are both positive attributes of human character, and efforts must be made to cultivate them in the children as well. Through regular discourses, he needs to be made clear that these attributes can always be used for the betterment of the society and it is always harmful when they are used as instruments or tool for self-gratification or subjugation. As mentioned earlier, these cannot be taught to a child in a single session. It is a practice that needs to be followed in a consistent manner. Cultivating these qualities requires discipline, time and patience.

Basically, the child must be allowed to grow in a way that typifies the situation what is required for a healthy childhood. As it is never possible to completely isolate the child from media violence, all these conscious practices can surely act as a guard or shield to protect the tender minds from the vicious attack of the myriad forms of violence depicted in the media.

The child must be encouraged to participate in a wide array of activities. Certain at-home activities like pursuing hobbies, exercising, making crafts, reading, playing games, tending the pets and helping out with household chores can be planned together with the child. A parent with a variety of interests can set a good example before the child.

The help of technology can be sought to control the child's exposure to violence. There are a lot of high-tech tools available that can aid the parents to monitor the programs watched by their children. For instance, the V-chip allows the TV programs to be monitored. It actually blocks the shows that have a high content of violence, sex or other aspects that are unsuitable for children. Then, certain channels can also be "locked out" by coordinating with the cable operators. The procedure is termed "scrambling" the channels or resorting to programmable remote controls, which the parents can override with a personal identification number. Other similar technologies can be used to filter Internet materials too.

Factors That Promote Violence

"The things you dwell on the most, you will end up indulging in."

You indulge in violence if you think of violence or are exposed to violence. In this regard, we can refer to the research stats stated in the Journal *Pediatrics*. Here the researchers from Dartmouth present this startling data. A huge number of adolescents are found increasingly exposed to the graphic violence depicted in films that are released with an R rating. These children belong to the age group of ten to fourteen. Out of the twenty-two million children in this age bracket, 12.5 percent of them watched these violent movies regularly. [28]

People have been acquainted with violence for centuries. But, in the modern society it has evolved as a serious threat as it has taken young minds in its inextricable grip. It has resulted in a deformation of children's outlook toward society and the manner in which they gets acquainted and understands their relations. These get manifested in the multitude of school shootings that take place from time to time and the rising rate of youth homicides. This is particularly in the context of the youth homicides. A child's mind is characterized as an extremely impressionable one. This fact and the conditions that they are exposed to, create an indelible impact on their psyche and influence their actions and behaviors. The child's surroundings in fact, offer definition to the person that he grows up into. This in turn defines the future of human society.[29]

So, it becomes of utmost importance to regulate and shape up the growing up environment as that alone will ensure a healthy childhood. The condition that a child finds himself in, for the major part of the day becomes a natural part of his system. He becomes psychologically adaptable to that particular situation.

This is basically a natural mode of adaptation of human behavior. In this process of acculturation, he begins to get accustomed to the attributes of the given situation. So, if it is a pleasant situation, the child will manifest the attributes characteristic of that condition. If it happens to be a violent situation, the qualities that are inherent, will be adapted by the child. As the child's mind is in a developing or an underdeveloped stage, his mind acts more like a piece of sponge. It readily absorbs the environmental qualities and starts to live with them and reflects the respective characteristics that mark it.

Over the last three decades, there have been numerous research studies focusing on the relationship between unusual adolescent behavior and exposure to violence. A direct correlation has been established in the studies, each distinctly marked as cross-sectional, longitudinal and experimental. [30]
It has been noticed that children who are below the age of four are unable to distinguish between fact and fantasy and they show an increased tendency to consider violence as a usual occurrence. In movies, particularly, violence is depicted as a

mode of conflict resolution. It is frequently depicted as consequential and effective means to attain the mission or objective.

The heroes receive awards and recognition for their violent behavior. Young minds begin to consider them as role models and they generate this belief that there is nothing wrong in "knocking off the bad guys". With enhanced and continuous exposure to these movies, they begin to consider violence as a righteous means that can be translated in their daily life and used as a means for retaliation against the perceived "victimizers". Regular exposure to violent movies and music make children desensitized regarding the negative impact of violence. Basically, they end up losing the ability to empathize with both the victim and the victimizer.

It has been observed that over fifteen percent of music videos depict inter-personal violence. [31] This is through the lyrics and even the mode of use of the orchestra. Music is often felt to be as a puritanical expression of art. This entails that a child develops this perception from the comment of his or her parents, elder members of the family, and teachers that music is something that helps in the spiritual development of the mind. Although, this s primarily with regard to the religious hymns, it also trickles down to other softer romantic numbers and various other modes of expressionist music.

If we look at the current musical genres available in the market, we would find that they hugely deviate from the conventional perceptions of music. The lyrics are deliberately made expressionist in terms of their graphic descriptions of themes that are unsuitable for comprehension by adolescent minds. Children and adolescents are simply not mentally equipped to endure the thought that these lyrics try to convey. Overt sexual connotations and detailed description of certain obsessive behaviors fall under this category of violence in both subtle and camouflaged forms.

When a child is exposed to lyrics, he or she usually generates the feeling that these descriptions and expressions are normal and can be readily incorporated into their daily behavior. The manner in which they begin to perceive relationships also is negatively affected by it. The usages of certain varieties of percussion instruments are also found to render certain impact on the tender minds. As they get 'used' to listening to these "musical" expressions of outrage, they naturally develop this feeling that the soft, soothing harmony is passé. They actually fail to distinguish between "rocking" and "entertaining". This leads to confused perceptions regarding the utility of music and the possible impact that it can cause on the human mind, especially during childhood.

Is violence inherent?

If it's not in you it won't come out of you.

This is a popular belief ingrained in majority of us. There are varied schools of thought in human psychology. According to a lot of thinkers and social analysts, the human mind is inherently adaptable. And, as a child has underdeveloped cognitive qualities, he or she is observed to "get into the feel" of his/her immediate environment just as a fish takes to water.

A child learns the characteristics of his surroundings and shapes accordingly. He/she is basically a representation of the environment.

Then again, it is also true that the human psyche is a composition of certain attributes that are more or less common to all. But, we find each individual as different. This is due to the fact that our personalities reflect a certain set of dominant qualities that actually define our characters. In other words, this is our "individuality"; some are compassionate, while some are indifferent, and then you have people who exhibit confused characteristics or some who are outright violent. Each of these characteristics can be used as means to determine the dominant conditions in which a respective individual grows up. Environmental conditions actually bring out those attributes that are conducive for that particular environment. Later on, we find that these very attributes form the defining characteristic of the respective individual. If the individual is exposed to violence, he or she will begin to accept it as a usual part of regular existence and accordingly resort to it in times of perceived need.

But again, there is another school of thought that states that we simply show those particular attributes that are inherent in us. This entails, that a person is not a composition of qualities; rather, he or she manifests only those that are actually present within him/her from birth. This basically disregards the statement that the environment highlights a certain section of qualities from the wide assortments of attributes that are present in each of us. In simple terms, if you have it in you, it will come out anyway; if you don't, there is no question of its external manifestation. So, if a child has a propensity to act violently, regardless of whether he or she is exposed to violence in the media, he or she will inevitably show violence in his behavior or activities. Likewise, if a child does not have this particular attribute, he or she will simply not exhibit violence. The established correlation between children resorting to violence and their exposure to violence, calls for necessary caution on the part of the parents.

Given below is a discussion of a few of the major sections in the form of questions and answers. You will enjoy them while recapitulating the important aspects of the lessons

Questionnaire:

1. How can television viewing be monitored?

Answer: Television is the most readily accessible form of media. Begin by charting out a routine for television viewing. It can be two hours or less per day. Sit with the child and plan out the programs and make sure to switch it off when the program gets over. Observe how the child relates to the content. Help him to understand situations that you feel are complex for a tender mind. Choose the programs carefully. Select those that are free from negative content.

2. How to ward off violence from music?

Answer: Music is a consumer product. As long as there are demands for a certain type of music, it will continue to be there on the racks. The elders need to guide the choices of the kids as they select their CDs and can render a vital influence through practice and teaching. The child needs to be taught on why music is helpful for the mental and psychological well-being of a person. Before exposing the child to a musical content, check the lyrics and the mode of orchestra used. Try to ensure that from the very beginning, it is the harmony and soothing characteristic of the lyrics that appeal to the child's mind. Pursue music as a relaxation only if the child has a natural inclination towards it.

3. How do role models promote violence?

Answer: Children have the tendency to create role models out of characters that they are attracted to. They have an inclination to have characters from films, cartoons, music videos, or TV series as their role models. The violence that is depicted in all these mediums render an impact on the impressionable minds of children. They try to enact the violence and develop the disturbing character traits as they grow up. Being unable to decide what is right or wrong for them, they do not understand the implications of their behavior. Not being aware of the consequences further complicates the situation. Basically, the inability to differentiate between the real and the imaginary or fantasy world makes them more vulnerable toward executing these acts of violence in their regular lives. This is how role models promote violence through the enactment of the same.

4. If a child is compassionate, does it entail that he would never be violent?

Answer: The character of a child is a follow through of the specific characteristics of his immediate environment. If he lives in a violence controlled environment, he would be naturally alien to the use of violence. But if he comes across violence in any form there are possibilities that he might adapt to the violence. This makes it important for the parents and elders to take care of the components of the immediate environment so as to make the growing up years of the child simple and enjoyable.

5. Choose the right option

The V-Chip helps to:
a. campaign against programs having violent content.

b. make the program go off air.

c. monitor the program.

d. none of these

Chapter 3: The Benefit of Using Rating

Children who are exposed to violence have been reported to display overtly aggressive behavior. In an attempt to alienate children from such harmful media content, strict implementation of restrictions becomes necessary. Rating television programs, films, Internet materials, and games can be very effective in demarcating the target viewer-ship. We have media content that caters to all sections of audiences and media products must be labeled so that they become easier to determine which are suitable for a young audience.

If we refer to the Children's Television Act or CTA in this regard, we will find that it has been quite instrumental in ensuring the airing of television programs that seek to meet the requirements of children. Commercial broadcast stations are actually compelled to air a minimum of three hours of programming that helps to further the educational and informational requirements of children below sixteen years of age. These programs particularly cater to a child's intellectual, cognitive, social, and emotional requirements. These educational objectives require the programs to berated "E/I" (Emotional Intelligence). They seek to foster cooperation and compassion through their programs.

Now, moving on to restrictive rating systems, the objective behind the rating system is to demarcate the content of the respective film, game or TV program actively in relation to the audience to whom it seeks to cater. Content ratings help parents to judge the content of a program prior to letting their children watch it. The mechanism of ratings is basically slated to act as warnings regarding the violent impact of harmful media content.

According to the American Psychological Association (APA), there is a direct correlation between the violent content of media (particularly television and to some extent films) and the increasingly aggressive behavior in children. In reference to the dreadful instances that are a direct follow-through of media violence, it is quite clear that our future generations are getting drowned in this world of inescapable violence. So, curbing and effectively restricting these natural human tendencies toward resorting to violence, particularly when the media acts as a provocateur, is of utmost importance. This is if we seek a healthy and sustainable existence of our human civilization.

There was a resolution passed by the APA informing the general public and broadcasters that there are potential dangers involved when the children are exposed to violence on television. It can be particularly relevant to discuss the research findings of Fulbright Professor Tasha Howe. In her lecture "Bang Bang, You're dead: How media violence affects children's development and behavior", in April, 2008, she stated that an average American child is exposed to 6.5 hours of screen media every day. [32]

This includes television, and computer and video games. According to the resultant stats, by age seventeen a teenager has witnessed around two hundred thousand violent acts, which includes forty thousand murders. As only 17 percent of parents keep a tab on the regulations, this violence reaches to these young children unfiltered. Thus, it would be advisable for parents to seek help by resorting to certain regulatory measures. The Entertainment Software Rating Board or The Movie Mom can effectively help the parents determine the rating of the violence in television programs. Once you begin to research on the possible regulatory measures, you will find more sources from sites like www.movierports.org.

According to child safety experts, cartoon shows must also contain movie-like ratings. If we consider the research of Dr. Karen Pfeiffer, a senior lecturer at Lincoln University, we will find evidence that there is a high probability of children resorting to risky behavior and ending up inflicting injuries on themselves after viewing certain violent cartoon programs. In the opinion of this international mentor for the World Health Organization, particular cartoon shows like Scooby-Doo, Batman, X-Men, and Ben 10 fall under this category. It is a similar problem in real life, as children are not able to understand the consequences of the violent acts; they get influenced easily. This calls for the need for ratings that would clarify the degree of portrayal of injury content for parents. This would enable them to make informed decisions. The enforcement of rating systems could effectively deny a child access to violence. The impact of violence in video games or any other audio visual mediums is specific to the right side of the human brain. The brain is not just a passive receiver (of the violent act or even a death caused by it) in this situation; rather, it is actively involved in inflicting the same upon another person. The majority of the readily available video games come with voluntary ratings, but we can conclude that the ratings have not been proved to be effective.

There have been suggestions of making a universal rating system for all media mandatory, which does not seem to be feasible. This is due to the fact that media is highly complex and the impact that it renders is also extremely varied. This actually calls for the development of multiple rating systems.

The rating system

The Motion Picture Association practices a rating system that seeks to provide advance information on the movies/shows for parents to decide whether or not they want their child to watch it. [33]

A "G" rating states that it is for General Audience, signifying that all ages are admitted. But, this does not mean that it is a children's film, as there could exist snippets of strong language. The violence is minimal and there are no scenes depicting nudity, sex, or usage of drugs.

A "PG" rating requires parents to decide on the appropriateness of the content for their children. It means parental guidance is necessary due to the mild presence of profanity, violence and/or brief nudity.

A "PG-13" rating signifies that parents ought to be strongly cautioned, as some materials in the movie may not suit children below thirteen. There are elements of adult activity, sensuality, language, nudity, and/or violence in them. The depiction of violence is not made extreme or persistent. Parents today usually are of the opinion that such elements and references to sexual context are inconspicuous.

An "R" rating means that it is restricted for viewers under seventeen and they must be accompanied by an adult guardian.

They contain adult themes, activities, hard language, intense and persistent violence, drug abuse, and/or sexual nudity.

With advancements in new media and other related social changes, the rating patterns have also undergone a change. Those films that were released with an R rating a decade age are released with a PG-13 rating today. It needs to be repeated here that the sole onus lies with parents to control and deny their children access to media violence.

Filtering

"To have a good output, filter the input".

It is a natural social requirement that our children grow up to be individuals who are equipped with rational understanding and able to decide on what is good for them and society at large. Being a part of the society, they must also be able to fulfill their obligations towards the society. This makes it important they we do our bit in ensuring that our future generations are not incapacitated from the desirable human attributes.

So, this again calls for the need of placing our children in an environment that is characterized with all the specific attributes that we dream or wish them to have. This actually calls for the regulation of the environment.

So, what do we infer from this discussion?

In an endeavor to realize this objective, it becomes imperative that we take adequate measures to ensure the appropriateness of the various media to which our children are exposed. Media in its multiple forms are increasingly found to depict violence in some form or another. The underdeveloped state of a child's mind is unwittingly exposed to the grisly attributes and the situation compounds as they try to present these violent acts in their daily lives. Persistent exposure to such harmful conditions actually results in their total delineation from characteristics like empathy and compassion, which are considered normal attributes in an ideal human being. They grow up to be lifeless individuals with little or no regard for emotional understanding. They become impatient and feel that violence is the accepted means to solve conflicts or attain the fulfillment of their desires. In the process, they indulge in methods that harm the safety of people residing in their immediate environment, apart from the immense loss that they cause to their own individuality. Numerous lives get lost through these events that are essentially the fall-out of the violent media exposure.

So, in order to allow children a normal, desirable future, we must check into the environment we are providing them. This entails that we filter the attributes that are actually harmful to the desired development of the young minds. Children watch movies and television series, which happen to be the most accessible medium of entertainment as well as information. Thus, it becomes the responsibility of the parents to check the exact content of these movies or TV series before they expose their children to them. This can be done through personally controlling the viewing time and programs along with taking a note of the ratings. The objectives of the ratings are to provide advance information on the content of the respective film or

TV series. It therefore, can be stated that these ratings actually act as filters to the wide assortment of information media that incessantly bombarded the generation today.

Here is an opportunity to rehearse the contents of the above chapter. You can take this as a summation of the major points.

Questionnaire

1. Why do children get readily influenced by violence on television?

Answer: Television today is a major part of a child's growing up years. There are numerous studies that indicate the direct relation between violence depicted on television and aggressive behavior in children. This is brought about by the violence in cartoon shows and the fictional incidents in series and even news. As the child can readily relate to the situation depicted on the television content, he feels that such acts of violence are regular in life. He imbibes them and considers it as a normal part of reality.

2. How is violence in cartoon harmful?

Answer: Apparently, cartoon shows are considered to be harmless but, there are certain content in those shows that have been found to make them a risky proposition for a child's psyche. Shows like the Scooby-Doo, X-Men or Ben 10 are found to have a lot of adult content and even shows like Tom & Jerry have a lot of violent sequences. These are mostly incorporated to induce humor but when the child starts to enjoy violence in a humorous manner, he also becomes insensitive towards the impact of violence.

3. How are ratings helpful?

Answer: Through the restrictive rating systems, one can actively limit the content of film, game, or TV programs in relation to the potential audience. The content ratings help parents judge the content of the program prior to letting their children watch it. The mechanism of ratings is basically slated to act as warnings regarding the violent impact of the harmful media content.

4. Is there any relevance in the difference between an "R" rating and a "PG-13" rating?

Answer: An "R" rating signifies that viewers over the age of seventeen can watch the content under parental guidance. A "PG-13" rating means that children under the age of thirteen are restricted from viewing the content. There are a certain degree of adult themes, nudity, sexuality and partial violence in these films. Even a few years back, those films released with an "R" rating are released today with a "PG-13" rating. The onus lies on the parents to filter the content and decide how they would like to expose their children to such films. This depends a lot on the mental maturity of the child.

5. Choose the right option
Through enforcing the ratings, the child
    a.   will not go to watch the film.

b. will bring the DVD home and watch it with his/her parents.

c. will have his/her parent will decide on the content before actually watching the film.

d. express his opinion so that the film-makers refrain from making disturbing pictures.

Conclusion

The impact of violence on young minds can render a worse impact in comparison to bullying. When a child is bullied, he is a victim of violence. Whereas, media violence can make a child an active participant in the situations that he/she indulges in after witnessing them on media. If children get used to aggressive behavior, their sensitivity toward the victims, who are sufferers of real life violence, lessens. Children, particularly those below the age of seven, need to be especially protected, as they fail to differentiate between fantasy and reality.

The most effective solution can be through adequate communication. Simply saying "You can't watch a violent show or game, as it is bad" will not work. The consequences of an action must be clearly explained. A child must be told that it is unrealistic that people can get away after committing a violent act. The children must be taught effective methods of conflict resolution. Verbal cruelty must be avoided too.

Finally, nothing can actually substitute the role played by the parents in solving this menace of media violence. Their actions practice and caution can alone render an indelible impact on a child's mind. The marketing of products that contain harmful content for children must be banned. This can be attained only through the willing participation of the respective audio-visual producers or the manufacturers of the video and computer games. The Children's Television Act that requires educational programming for the broadcasters must be strictly enforced. Thorough research, including surveys, can lead to the drafting of other necessary legislations which aim to implement the desired controls and ratings.

It is also the responsibility of the respective media outlets to present content that are readily accessible to children in a manner that they do not end up harming their underdeveloped psyche. The random acts of violence or criminal activities ought to be discussed in a manner that is totally desensationalized so that children do not cultivate a sense of fear regarding a certain section or community.

Bibliography

Reference Links/Links of Interest:

[1] http://health.howstuffworks.com/teenage-brain1.htm

[2] http://en.wikipedia.org/wiki/Prefrontal_Cortex

[3] http://en.wikipedia.org/wiki/Synapses

[4] http://en.wikipedia.org/wiki/Myelin

[5] http://en.wikipedia.org/wiki/Nucleus_accumbens

[6] http://findarticles.com/p/articles/mi_m1590/is_4_58/ai_79967172/

[7] http://health.howstuffworks.com/teenage-brain2.htm

[8] http://www.triassociation.org/newsletter/highlights/09/adolescent_brain.htm

[9] http://health.howstuffworks.com/teenage-brain2.htm

[10] http://www.mediaawareness.ca/english/issues/violence/effects_media_violence.cfm

[11] http://health.howstuffworks.com/teenage-brain2

[12] http://www.killology.org/stanfordstudy.htm

[13] www.suite101.com/article.cfm/media_literacy/42205

[14] www.termpaperdownloads.net/sample1.htm

[15] http://www.mediaawareness.ca/english/issues/violence/violence_entertainment.cfm

[16] www.mediafamily.org/facts/facts_music.shtml

[17] http://www.thestar.com/entertainment/article/419019

[18] http://www.timesonline.co.uk/tol/news/uk/article2584819.ece

[19] http://news.aol.com/main/nc/article/more-arrests-in-homecoming-gang-rape-in/737532

[20] http://www.smh.com.au/news/technology/teens-arrested-over-rape-video/2008/09/11/1220857715493.html

[21] http://www.lazygamer.co.za/general-news/media-blames-another-senseless-killing-on-videogames/

[22] http://www.zurinstitute.com/teenviolence.html#shootings

[23] http://www.trutv.com/library/crime/serial_killers/weird/kids1/index_1.html

[24] http://www.thestar.com/entertainment/article/419019

[25] http://www.mediafamily.org/facts/facts_vlent.shtml

[26] http://www.mediafamily.org/facts/facts_vlent.shtml

[27] http://www.medialit.org/reading_room/article15.html

[28] http://www.sciencedaily.com/releases/2008/08/080804100150.htm

[29] http://www.mediafamily.org/facts/facts_vlent.shtml

[30] http://www.aacap.org/cs/root/developmentor/the_impact_of_media_violence_on_children_and_adolescents_opportunities_for_clinical_interventions

[31] http://www.mediaawareness.ca/english/issues/violence/violence_entertainment.cfm

[32] http://nicosia.usembassy.gov/EmbatWork/ViolenceTalkApr08.htm

[33] http://en.wikipedia.org/wiki/Motion_Picture_Association_of_America_film_rating_system

Selective Readings:

1) Bryant, Jennings, David Roskows-Ewoldsen, and Joann Cantor, eds. *Communication and Emotion: Essays in Honor of Dolf Zillmann.* Muhwah, NJ: Lawrence Erlbaum Associates, 2003.
2) Carter, Cynthia and C. Kay Weaver. *Violence and the Media.* Philadelphia: Open University Press, 2003.
3) Goldstein, Jeffrey. *Why We Watch: The Attractions of Violent Entertainment.* New York: Oxford University Press, 1998.
4) Hoffman, Allan, M., ed. *Schools, Violence and Society.* Westport, CT: Praeger, 1996.
5) Langone, John. *Violence!: Our Fastest-Growing Public Health Problem.* Boston: Little Brown, 1984.

6) Loeb Adler, Lenore and Florence L. Denmark. *Violence and the Prevention of Violence.* Westport, CT: Praeger, 1995.

7) Moeller, Thomas G. *Youth Aggression and Violence: A Psychological Approach.* Mahwah, NJ: Lawrence Erlbaum Associates, 2001.

8) Osofsky, Joy D. *Children in a Violent Society.* New York: Guilford Press, 1997.

9) Palmer, Edward L. and Brian M. Young, eds. *The Faces of Televisual Media: Teaching, Violence, Selling to Children.* Muhwah, NJ: Lawrence Erlbaum Associates, 2003.

10) Pirog-Good, Maurine and Jan E. Stets, eds. *Violence in Dating Relationships: Emerging Social Issues.* New York: Praeger, 1989.

11) Ury, William, ed. *Must We Fight? From the Battlefield to the Schoolyard, a New*

Perspective on Violent Conflict and Its Prevention. San Francisco: Jossey-Bass, 2002.

12) Zimmering, Franklin E. *American Youth Violence.* New York: Oxford University Press, 1998.

13) Zimmering, Franklin E. and Gordon Hawkins. *Crime Is Not the Problem: Lethal Violence in America.* New York: Oxford University Press, 1999.

CPSIA information can be obtained
at www.ICGtesting.com
Printed in the USA
LVHW021130200921
698243LV00002B/261